STONE RUN: *Tidings*

STONE RUN: Tidings

by Cynthia Grenfell

Decorations by Dennis Culver

Sunstone Press
Santa Fe, New Mexico

FIRST EDITION. Printed in the United States of America

Library of Congress Cataloging in Publication Data:

Grenfell, Cynthia, 1930–
    Stone run: tidings.

    I. Title.
PS3557.R4385S8   1983   811'.54   83-398

ISBN: 0-86534-023-4

Published in 1983 by SUNSTONE PRESS / PO Box 2321 / Santa Fe, New Mexico 87501

CONTENTS

Why, why is it? Why so rude before?
But between the shouting and the sulking
There is struggling to be born
A creature of calm
One who knows
And who does not yet know love

This world is soon not my world
Certain things are coming forth
From my past and present
Full of meaning:
Things not me now, and yet
A part of me still, as I am part of them
> *Gardens*
> *Friendship*
> *The fleeting breath of air called song*
> *Child, children, anybody's*
> *Mountain, seashore*
> *You*
And the most important of these will be love

PART ONE

I pause, leaving my camp, at
A circular pile of rocks
Concave
Grown over with bunch grass
And yucca
Next to this old trail
Here on the mesa

How large a house
Would a man need
Living on a breezy mesa
Facing north?
Did he build it
Just large enough to lie in
His cookfire in the lee?
Did he haul up mud
For plaster from the spring below?
Was it for year-round or just summer?
Was there any shade back then?

If there'd been any real trees
Big enough for shade
He'd of made a cabin
Of logs

But it was stone

And here the remains lie
Fallen in
Scant wildflowers for its garden
Dreams blown away in
The west wind

Were there two living here?
Placer-kings
Miners
Sand-sifters
Of the hot arroyos

The gold was here

Most of them lived
Up at Dolores
This hut and the few others
Like it on these rock aprons
Must have been made by
Mavericks of mavericks
Did they find town life confining?
Were they tossed out?
Was it a desire to live closeby
Their sandpiles?

What a horrendous event
When the floodrains came
And the torrents rushed
Down the arroyos
Washing the work and the world away
Swamping the sands
Secreting and revealing
Bringing new nuggets
From above

Mighty men and their
Mighty dreams
Are the ones most often sung
But these outskirt joes
As they drifted through
Left a trace of lost and won

In this region of transition
Not the northern forests
Not quite the plains
Or the deserts of the south
One of those crotchety
Alien places
That caught the debris of the ages
Out of the ordinary
In its faults
Gold and turquoise and silver
Spaceworks
Cached in the back pockets
Of the universe
Treasure hidden away
Found in unconformities
By non-conformists

For these hard men
Seeking the wonders and the answers
The starscent of riches
Sparkling behind their eyes
How would it be?

Not chaos but
All things possible
Effortlessly balanced
Ever in flow. Vacancies filled.

Look at a rain forest
Jungle growth
Everything that can be here, is here.
Even me.
Abundantly.

How did a hammock get its name?
An area of ground
Imperceptibly swaying
A few feet above the surrounding
Wetlands
Cypress, pine, palm, liana,
Bromeliad, fern, live oak:
Examples of its obvious flora.

A portion of drier land
Elevated from the swamp.

We tour the boardwalk
Through the Hammock Park near Canaveral
Watching for egrets, moccasins, porcupines
And anything between.
Watching for our ghosts
Primaeval, perpetual,
Recalling to mind certain cell-memories
Stirring in our very bones.
Silent as a caught breath
     Habitat waiting
We feel eyes probing our backs
Wondering if we intend to stay
And what accommodation will be made.

The hammock is at ease in its precise awareness
Drawing automatically into transition,
Forever,
The was, is, and will-be;
Demonstrating that all is here,
That it is
All the same.

TWO SCENES

Porpoise sleekly rolling, arching
Swimming shallow by the boat
People peering, cameras clicking
Mama, baby, black and white
Nine in all, gleaming, flashing
Spirits of Pacific deep
Rarely known and now appearing
Gracious, eager, welcoming

*

Fat-ruffled rufous hummer
Early day before the sun
Out patrolling, preening, buzzing
Even me who fills his jar
Do beware! small bugs a-winging
He will grab you in a gulp
Other hummers, keep your distance
For he is all-vigilant

Now a whir of aerial combat
Lances thrust and curses screamed
Challenge of an emerald broadtail
Bigger than the chunky red
Flinging all around the garden
In a duel of tiny missiles
Mighty battle of the bottle
Whose tree is this, anyway!

JUNCO SONG

The last of the juncos
Departed here today
    Kitty-neece
    Kitty-naughty
    Kitty-neece
In the tummy, beak and feathers
Of my pretty predator
    Kitty-neece
    Kitty-naughty
    Kitty-khat

All have gone to the northlands
With their tails perking white
    Kitty-neece
    Kitty-naughty
    Kitty-neece
But this last dilly-dallied
Was devoured beak and feathers
    Kitty-neece
    Kitty-naughty
    Kitty-khat

Little flock of the winter
Gaily churpt on the ground
    Kitty-neece
    Kitty-naughty
    Kitty-neece
Easy catching, easy eating
For my little feather-breath
    Kitty-neece
    Kitty-naughty
    Kitty-khat

Creatures' ways do surprise us
Claw and fang, beak and feather
    Kitty-neece
    Kitty-naughty
    Kitty-neece
It's their nature to be knowing
Strong the kingdom between
    Kitty-neece
    Kitty-naughty
    Kitty-khat

THE PUFFING TREE

This morning
Pollen puffs
In sunlight
Mulberry tree spits
Tiny explosions
Dangling garlands
Springing tassels
Blooming fringe

Sturdy little tree
Growing fast
These three years now
It's "seedless" (guaranteed)

Its spring display
Nevertheless
Perpetuates
The celebration
Of the being of its
Every cell

To cerebrate
Continually
Is not for me

I watch the creatures
I plant cabbages
Tend the roses
Feel the breeze

I am in fact
Delighted
That my hands
Find work
Crochet, sew
My fingers know
Some secrets of
Spring babies.

A mild and mellow
Mood today
Storms are
Somewhere else
The chickens call
The kittens play
Mulberry tosses
Its exuberant pollen
Onto quiet air
Scent of lilac
Pulse of rootlets
Probing

Bumbling schoolbus
Punctuating

COMPLAINT

The iris are mine
And the glorious poppy
The roses
But why the aphids?

Atalaya is mine
The knitting is mine
My neighbors are mine

The slowness of the seeds
In the ground
To germinate
Is also mine

Chester is lake water
Her eyes are the exact luminous pale green
Her pied pelt is the speckled
Brown, grey, black
Of water flowing over
Sand, gravel, stones
Her white gives the purity and clarity
Of the water itself
The pink of her tiny nose reminds me
Of little fishes and other little beings
Like, perhaps, shrimp, or snails' undies
Little soft fleshy inquisitive creatures
That might inhabit a stream
A miniature crab, maybe.

Her softness, silkiness resembles
The liquid itself
Ongoing through the pool
The slippery, almost unperceived
Mystery of
The gentle persistence of its seeking
To the ocean

Her spottiness is the dappling
Of reflected trees

Her energy
Her vast resource of play
Her unconscious, instinctive work
Of killing
Part of nature's pattern
Is like the work of the water
As it descends along its path.
Not self-directed, it naturally
Follows where it falls; and
If impeded
Relentlessly accumulates power
To break through whatever barriers.

I remember streams of childhood

Beechmont Lake
Fed by the extraordinary
Rock filled
Pool shapen
Murmuring
Slick gushing
Fauna flourishing
Sunsplashed
Common everyday
Brook

Sneaker-soaked, we netted
Pre-frog jelly masses
Bringing them home in jars.
Deprived of the constant nourishment
Of the living stream
They always perished.

I peer into Chester's eyes
Fondle the luxuriant fur

For a long moment
Motionless
Suspended between ticks of the clock

We are the stream
We are in the stream, of the stream
We are the stream
I am the flow
I am the black and white pebbles

I am caressed, I caress
I feel not the wetness but
The fluid rhythm of a smile
The tumble of the molecules
Through me, of me
In their good-humored jostling
Stretching, curling

Sunwarmed
The skin on my back
As I sit here in the bay window
Prickles slightly

The cat on my lap
Has gone to sleep

Corn and radishes
The summer she was seven
Corn and radishes
That summer at camp

Her first camp
That hard summer

It seemed all they ate
Was corn
At the long dining tables
As the hot sun slanted in
Corn and more corn
Sweet and buttery
Rolled in salt
Sticky crystals
At that place she
Was sent
After her father left her

She never looked at papers
When he died
Fearing to see his pictured
Face, forbidden to her
Round-spectacled solemn eyes
Glaring at her
Accusing her

There had been a ripping wail
Of grief from the upstairs
Bedroom
She heard it break through the
Open windows quickly closed
As she loitered in the
Garden below
On the path from the
House to the barn
Gravelly
Under gnarled old dogwoods

The cry and sobbing
From their room
Shuddered her
Turned her to ice
Made her bones wobble
She sank to the ground
And lay silent
Hating
Condemning herself
Silently begging him not to go
That she didn't mean it
She didn't mean it
It can't be true
Why did this happen to her
How could he do this to her

They shut her away from
The hurt, shielding her
No funeral, no mention
Of his name
    Her father
Who played the piano
As she would drift to sleep
Evenings
    Her father
Who came home on the
Commuter train
She jumped up and down
To see him
    Her father
Who had a bad heart
And did not extend
Himself
She tried to win him
To earn his love
He disappeared

The camp was found
For her, to keep her away
And so she became
Doubly distanced

The silent order was
To forget him
With him gone
Her first seven years
Of this life were erased also

Obedient, she accepted
With eyes lowered
She displaced herself
Did what was asked and
Went unmurmuring to the
Camp
Held the fresh-pulled radishes
Under the tap, laughing
At their stinging hotness
Rode in the buggy
Swam in the lake
Sang the songs

Apart from the others
Lest they notice her oddness

Clutching her agony
And her anger
Where no one would see

Ate corn and corn and
Corn
Choking on corn
All that summer
Her seventh summer
All those years ago
In all that time
She never knew about
Missing those first years.

Was she a warm, loving
Child? How very long
It has taken to open
Her heart, even a bit
To ask to know again
That little girl
To accept, love and cherish her
And say perhaps, with a
Smile and a nudge,
It's all right, you can
Come home now

DID YE KNOW?

LAKE HAMILTON, DAY AFTER EASTER

O sunny morn
O wisped sky
Oak trees in bloom
Goldgreen leafy, long-legged

More of water in my dream
Flowing gently
Dark and quiet
Where once a meadow flashed
With creatures' morning walks.

O drowsy mountain
Over north, or south
Whichever your regard
Ancient Ouachita

Voices no more to raise
Shouting and laughing
Of those dead to this world

Drone of small boat motor
Lap of small wave on pebbled shore
Web of black spider
A reminder
Of a small boy
Known from pictures
If he ever was

IN PAN'S WORLD

In Pan's world
Where he and I dwelt
Unbelief ebbed
And things were what they
Seemed
We rejoiced together
He and I
In our happiness and pain
And our words were real
Ideas were truths
Innocent, lacking fault
Faith-full, beloving
Expressing essential godliness

In this world
Machines shock
Souls sting
Words sly-pose

Which way over the mountain
Does the yellow bird
Fly?

LAMENT

My love come back!
Whether by the arrow gleameth
Or more slowly
Seeping as water through old wood
I need you!
Yearning to you in my dark black habit
Hope of you fails
Why does my hurt heart
Reject its own?
Sour tears feedeth no child

No other one on earth
No other song
But yours

My love come back!
Are you lost forever?

CONEFLOWER GROUNDCOVER

With this world springing to life
    Why is she gone?
Beautiful entity
Having chosen form of cat
    White buff silver
    Innocent predator
    Endearing
    Essence of tidy
    Tiny beguiler
    Huntress
Whither didst thou wander?
Why did you seek a path away?

My brain leaps for air
It flutters and stalls
Pictures and images whiz through
    Which I can't follow
    Barely see
    Laughing at my slow awareness
    Flirting and flashing
Borne of themselves
Showing off, parading behind my retina
    A kaleidoscope
    Of dreams forgot and yet to come
    (In our terms)

The book I read deals with death-of-cat
On this very page of a week ago
When Chester left
    Did she not know I'd return?

As we paused in the graveyard Easter Day
Gardenias to place by the stones
    Of lover-husband-father and son-brother
    Gone these years...

Was there something in her of them?
A reminder to love
A remembrance to see through the tears
A memory re-stirred as my heart is rent
    For so many tenants
    So many loves
    I mention and miss and mourn
    Who were and will be born

Dry barren-seeming winter ground
Smells sweet with ages of memories
Bird-blood let; linnet heart-song
A tasty morsel lost on the etheric
Sunlit
Time to nest again
Time for sprouts of coneflower
Peeping forth in diminutive forest
A mantle to cover the desert
A natural invasion
Army of tiny greenstems
Sprung from the mythical blood and bones
Of feather and fur and twig

It is all one

And yet
As I watch the lion in the grass
Knowing he and his kind will
Also vanish from our temporal view

And the arms yearn to hold
The lips to caress
The heart leap with recognition
In identity

My tears do flow
In mourning

I know the sprigs are coneflower
You see, because I
Recognize them from my memory
Of my local flora
From last year

Would that
My temporal friends, sons and lovers
Return.

NOT READY

What we are not ready to hear
Or to understand
The knowing that will
Shelter us like
An endless canopy
And does indeed cover us now
We are not aware of
Consciously

Yet there is the high sweet
Ringing in our ears
And some of us hear the voices

And there is beauty

Until the time when all is
Revealed
Until the time when we will see
And know in a flash

Our restless minds see not
The beckoning
There is no need
Yet

The family fields are growing
The family fields are growing
   Giggling girlies
   Dancing parties
   Pretty babies
The family fields are growing

      I sit here without knowing
      I sit here without knowing
      How family fields are growing
      Pretty babies, pretty girls

The crops are soon for harvest
The crops are soon for harvest
   Corn, asparagus
   Beans, lettuce
   Nasturtiums, peas
The crops are soon for harvest

The cats are mouse a-prowling
The cats are mouse a-prowling
   Chickens scratching
   Water pumping
   Cows a-mooing
The cats are mouse a-prowling

The babies of the springtime
The babies of the springtime
   Yawn and suckle
   Fair as flowers
   Bits of Heaven
The babies of the springtime

We all shall eat this winter
We all shall eat this winter
   Hard potatoes
   Dried bananas
   Luscious pears
We all shall eat this winter

We shall rejoice in darkness
We shall rejoice in darkness
  By the fire
  In the blankets
  Telling stories
We shall rejoice in darkness

The stories tell of heroes
The stories tell of heroes
  Riding horses
  Making music
  Sailing clouds
The stories tell of heroes

The heroes made the magic
The heroes made the magic
  For the planting
  For the dancing
  For the chanting
The heroes made the magic

The magic is the loving
The magic is the loving
  Fills our hearts
  Fills our stomachs
  Fills our arms
The magic is the loving

We wonder in the telling
We wonder in the telling
  Native rhythms
  Of our wholeness
  Holy temples
We wonder in the telling

We all shall sing together
We all shall sing together
  The old sagas
  In the circles
  Of the sacred
We all shall sing together

It happens in the old ways
It happens in the old ways
  Crazy circles
  All around us
  Really heartforms
It happens in the old ways

And no one needs the knowing
And no one needs the knowing
  Words are water
  Bubbling brightly
  From the well-spring
And no one needs the knowing

BLACK / WHITE

My chickens were all black and white
And white and black striped
Barred
My dog in childhood (Hector)
Black and white
My best horse (Bandit)
Black and white
My first cat (Pootie)
Black and white

One day when I got my
Second cat, Chester,
Thinking her to be black and white
I found, when I could catch and caress her,
For she was very much afraid,
That she was white, black and grey.
As she matured she became
White, black, grey and buff.
She wore a sky blue
Patent leather bell-collar.
The birds she caught and ate
(Except for a few tell-the-tale feathers)
Were almost all grey birds,
Occasionally a (and I weep for this
In exasperation)
Bluebird

She disappeared
To my great regret
While I was gone on a pilgrimage
When I returned
She had left me

Meanwhile
I acquired more chickens
Silver-grey and
Orange
Another kitten
To curl up in the nest left by my beloved Pootie
Was thrust into my arms
He is beige
And grey. He is Rannix

My new kitty needed
Company
When Chester left
So Fuega came to live with me
Also
She is
White, black and puregold

Nevertheless, I still have my first
Black and white hen, Dolores
Of the elegant egg
And jetblack
Alice-Blue-Gown

VERBATIM I

Wonderland
However
All the same things
As in the dreams:
Chickens, fences
Flowers in the trees
Friendly hand opens
Smiling faces
All good wishes
Answered

Why a connection
Here? It is too hot.
A little still bus will
Take us
All around
Don't buy the
Second part also
Of children again
Playing

I have a code
With myself
A guide of signals
Symbols
While asleep
Sometimes I pay
Attention
And sometimes not

PART TWO

THE SCULPTURE GARDEN

Here is a sculpture garden
At the entrance to my house
> *Not my home but*
> *A house which I own*
I stroll among countless nudes
Roman-style
At every turn of my foot
Gleaming, delicate
Perfect in all details
> *Their stances are athletic*
> *Sensuous*
> *Authentic*
> *The motion is frozen*
I wonder
Puzzled, why these
People, caught in stone
Men
> *Polished surfaces glistening*
> *As if with sweat*
And women
> *Lightly robed*
> *Displaying their various riches*
Are made to repeat
The same lives and problems
Over and over
> *Tedium, tedium*
> *Thus the bored expressions*
> *Run down*
> *With old rusted parts*
Caught skillfully
By the sculptors
(The artists within
Themselves)
In their everyday
Actions, intimate
And heroic
> *Caught in a web*
> *With no struggle*
Their vacant faces
Revealing nothing
Of their minds
> *Posing*

*   *   *

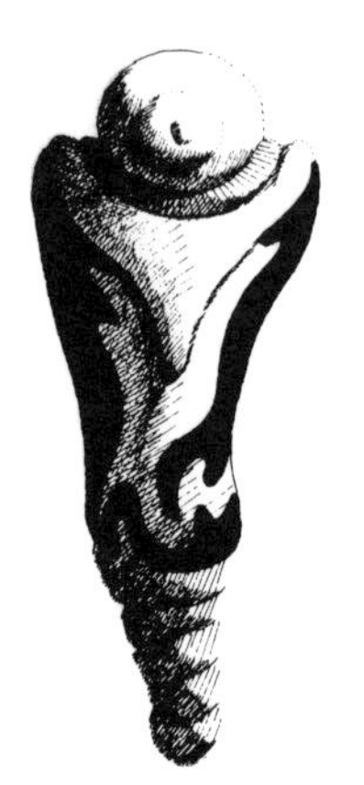

Behind the house
Squats a vulgar
Potting shed
Vernacular-built
Unlike the many-storied
Mansion
With the garden
>*This place seeds and nurtures*
>*For the front*
Off to the side
Safe within a small
Thicket of brushy
Wild plums
>*Undisturbed*
Where the gardener
>*An old Hag of Winter*
>*Bent of back*
Labours lovingly every spring
Easily working her magic

The tender green plants
Are ready
To be stuffed into
The still-rich soil
Of the garden
To manifest their spirits
Joyously
>*They are fresh and leafy*
>*Vibrant, sturdily grown*
>*With marble-size fruits*
>*In the bud*
Eagerly they thrust
Their delicate white roots
Into the prepared
Well-mulched ground
>*Forming a many-knotted seine*
These plants are the lives
Of the stone people
Who regard them not
>*Beguiled as they are*
>*In the slow-dance to*
>*Someone else's tune*
The statues hear not
Their own song

THE CATS OF TIME

The cats of time are waiting
Feed us feed us they ask.
Black, and yellow-striped.
From Egypt, earlier.
All quiet, dark, cold.
I step down on the patio from the snug house.
A cow mourns for her calf.
No moon, no stars
All rain and mist.

They wait, under the bushes
 Below the dripping leaves
 In their tiny cavelets
To be fed.

VERBATIM III

I'm attaching row after row
Of gauze panels
For a vulgar man.

An insect
Comes around
I kill him

Saving a lot of biting
And bloodshed

It is beautiful
And airy
Like wings

HOT NIGHT

1   Fairy wheels
    Dandelion wands
    Bushy treats in the fields

    Where withall
    Withheld
    Belong instead

    To Mary's ghost
    In strange patches
    Of moonlight

2   Done can bring
    To fruiten
    May blossoms

    Silver berries
    Of wry thoughts
    Tingling

    Not bells
    But wheels
    Of cymbling chariots

3   Juggling companions
    Skittering
    In the dark

    Unlit paths
    Brambling
    Thistly

    Scrambling
    To the bank
    Of the stream

4   Where are treetops
    Hustling pushing
    Shouldering

    In the nightwind
    Crowding
    Peering

    Tiny footprints
    Snakelet sand-
    Slithering

5   To the lapping
    Edge of water
    Drinking deeply

    Watchful
    Listening
    Cooled

    Dark inhabit
    Dabbling briefly
    Surfeit

TRIO

Four twilight-robed figures
Suspended from a line
Stretched above a wall
Of stone, smooth and rounded
Like polished mudbricks
Hung from a cord
Silvery thin
Reaching left and right
Into the mysteries of eternal
Being both ways

A feeling they were male
Once, that now it is no
Difference. Heavy and solid
Yet flappy in the night wind
Dandling
In the dull darkness
Like storm clouds hovering
On the mesa horizon

Mute, inevitable, indifferent
Oppressively apparent
Even with the eyes
In the back of your head
String an arrow in your bow
And shoot them; pierce
Their hooded unseen faces
With your skilled stroke
They will tumble one by one
And roll noiselessly down
The sloped side of the canyon
Piling up amidst the boulders
Like more of that kind
Scattered in the bed
Of the ancient dry stream
Flowing for the Rain Ceremony
Once in a long day

You watch the robots fall
As you stand in the canyon
Gazing along the precipice
You are lithe and supple
Saliva drools from your lips
Eager to suck their wounds
Dry of blood
Your quivver, tassel'd
And feather'd, chafes not
Your sweating back. You
Are accustomed to the hunt
These, the looming ones
The presences
Are your usual prey

Even as you kneel and crouch
Relishing the saltiness
The rich-iron tang
Running from the open places
The gathering comes again
From beyond that horizon
That last mountain range
Whose passes have denied your feet

Your danger and your supply
Your source
The awesome nest of the goddess
Hovering in past dreams
You barely recall

Even as you lie down
Surfeit and somnolent
Covering your nakedness
For shelter
With the soiled stuff of the robes
And drift to sleep
Without a pang, forgetting
Your own dragons
Waiting gleefully for you to cross over
To your private lands,

Above, on the mesa rim
Shuffling, murmuring
In the stillness
Without a breath of air drawn
Or released, but now withheld
Four looming figures
Are taking their places
Suspended from a fragile line
Hulking
Hung by the giant hands
Of the invisible workers
Of consciousness
The supply is endless
And unfathomable
Ten become a thousand in
The blink of an eyelid
Tapping into secret scaffolds
The silver nails of hints
And reasons

And in the dust of the canyon floor
The pebbles and boulders
Arrange themselves
Into the very foundation
Of the great construction
While to you they are but
Obstacles to climb around

*
*

Who speaks through me?
Says the shaman
All night waiting, watching
Handling the correct sacred objects
Singing the immemorable chants
The fairy-fires gleaming all around;
What message passes through
And who is it for?
The gentle stirring of his night air
Causes a rustle of maple leaves
Above his forest floor circle of
Round stream-washed stones
No campfire: it is he who
Centers the magic circle
Praying for his muse

High above, a fitful southeast wind
Blows heavy clouds
Yellow-brown, curling and folding
Pregnant with disaster
They bulge below
Their droppings engorging
Fragile water sacs
Tension unsteady as they
Are bullied about
Crossly by urgent gusts

They will not hurl their load
On the shaman
Or his forest world
Directly
They wait for the far northern
Wastes, so-called
Steppes, tundras, ice-masses
Where the ongoing vast spiral
Will crunch ahold of the particles
And fling the fragments off in turn
To cover the whole known world
Spinning above, below
In contrary motion
The very ions of the poison
Seeping into the living cells

*Says the shaman
There is work to be done
Here and now:
Yet my mind knows not what
Nor how. My garment is
Sundered, the banner is
On the stake
The seed is laid in crescents
Just so
And the spring water
Is in the precious-green jar
My mind is stilled
But no voice is heard
The stars are hidden by
Clouds so high no eye can see them
The messages are not coming
Through, and I must
Wait*

      *

      *

      *

*The woman, clutching her skirts up
Around her thighs
Steps from rock to rock
Through the gurgling brook
Flowing effortlessly over
And around boulders and pebbles
Of the canyon
Descending from the
Heights of the mountains
To the north*

*It is not a
Dangerous crossing, for the
Water is low and
The smooth rounded stones are
Steady.
Her child waits on the
Far bank
Eager to be off to the meadow
Where grow the tall bushes
With the purple berries
Baskets in both hands
He jumps up and down
Urging her to hurry
Laughing with her as
She teeters, pretending to
Slip. Then with a small leap
She is on the bank
And they scurry up the way
Pounded by countless feet
Up the little cliff
To the grassy field they must now cross
Running, racing and
Burbling in their pleasure
And anticipation of the feast
They will bring
Back to the camp*

The passerby
On his journey
To the sea
Becomes
The main actor

Before him
Drooping from one foot
A man
Recently dead
Hangs in a steel-
Frame tower

Mercy mercy
On his soul
Cries the young
Traveler
Bone weary and
Dusted from
Head to foot
With fine sands
And particles
From the paths
He has trod

I shall call for
Help to
Cut him down
We shall give him
Decent burial
Here in this
Desolate place

He then climbs
Up the steel tower
Where there is
A broadcasting
Transmitter

But it is bringing
Messages in
And he cannot
Send one out
To call for help
For someone to come
Cut down the man
Hanging under
The tower

He hears the faint
Buzzing of the
Space songs and
Wonders
What kind of language
The space creatures
Speak in
He understands
Nothing
And wishes they would
Fall silent

He clings to his
Dilemma and
Waits, looking
Around at the
Landscape

From where he
Perches, near the
Top, he can see
In all directions
Far back in the
Way he came from
The mountains
Huddle dimly
Barely visible in
Mists and clouds
He thinks of the
Long path stretching
From there to here

He gazes the other way
And to his amazement
Realizes that on
The horizon
Still many days walk
Lies the ruffling sea
The goal of his journey
His decided destiny
Although he cannot see it
Clearly
Its grey presence is
Unmistakable
From all he's heard
Of it
Birds flying in
From that direction
Are calling his name
They bear saltiness
On their wings
And pause on the tower
To clean and groom
Themselves
He smells the brininess
Wafting toward him

He knows that
When he gets there
He will plunge into
The water
Headlong
Swimming like a
Mackerel
Sleekly silver
Gleefully
He will glide
Across the bottom
Of the ocean
To the other shore
Far far away
And back
Without stopping
Refreshed
Cleansed
Alive

Then, beaching
On the near shore
The one he senses
From up here on the
Tower
He imagines himself
Exhausted, replete
Satisfied
His body worn out

The green-mossed
Halves of his skin
As he lies heaving
Separate
Like the twin
Shells
Of a blooming
Poppy
Like those in the field
Below
Revealing
His brilliant
Diamond clear
Gleaming essence

Alive as the hanged man
Is dead below him
Whipping and flicking through
All the schools
And ancient wrecks
Scanning the seafloor
Slipping among the
Seaweeds
Slithering past the
Eels and sharks
Out-swimming them
All

Then his mind-picture
Evaporates
Evanesces into
The air surrounding
The tower
There is a soft sag
As it leaves him and
His mind returns
From all that distance
Back into his
Awake head
Now he has come
Back into himself
Yet he remembers
How it was in
The ocean
And how good
It felt to be
Free

The young man
Sways slightly
And thinks about
Getting down
Off the tower
Not looking at
The man hanging
From the frame
Passing by him
With his head
Turned

And continuing
On his path
To his destination
For now
He knows new eagerness
For where he
Is going

A mockingbird alights
Next to him
Clinging to the frame
As he clings
And tilts her grey
Head
Peering at him
With a shoebutton eye
Taking her arrival
As a sign
He stares back
Mutely
Hoping to receive
Her message

No raven I
He feels her say
Nor dove
I sing many songs
And call in
Divine languages
Giving pleasure
Besides
With a blink and
A white-flashed wink
Of her tail
She flies off

Reuben Reuben
The young man shouts
I been thinking -
And he becomes
Very strong
As lightly as a
Down-feather
He floats
Earthward
Stopping by the
Deadman
To loosen him
And bears him
Easily
To the ground

He lays the body
Lovingly
On its side
And draws up
The cold limbs
In the old way
And stands above it
With his hands
On his hips
Not knowing what
To do next

I cannot dig a grave
For I have no shovel
I cannot bury it
For I have no flame
I cannot put it in the river
For there is no river
I cannot bear to
Leave these old bones
Here unattended
For this was once a
Temple of a soul
And must be treated
With respect
And reverence

Then a trembly voice
Hard on the edges
Speaks to him saying
I am the soul of this
Body and I am lost
I left this mass
Of blood and bone
Unhappily
By violence
Two days ago
And have been wandering
Ever since
I know not which
Way to go

The young man suggests
Can you not
Climb up to the
Top of the tower
As I did
And look in
All directions
I saw the mountains
Where I came from
And the sea
Where I'm going

Whining, the voice
Speaks again
This time flinging
Past the young man's
Shoulder like a petulant
Fart

I don't want to go
To the sea nor
The mountains
I want to go
Straight up
To the stars
Where I came from
How can you presume
To know where a
Soul
Is journeying?

The young man answers
Yes but I've been on
Imagination trips
And I think it's
Somewhat like...

No it is not
Snaps the soul
Of the dead body
Quit arguing
You know nothing

I know I've opened
A can of worms
Cries the young man
The soul does not answer
For it has gone
On its way
Spiralling skyward
As on a thermal
Briefly
Then dropping
With a thump
Like a heartbeat
Into another field
To the north

Well maybe this old body
Will tell me
What to do
He says
As he watches it
Hoping for a
Response

It says nothing
And does less
The young man
Sits down to wait
And think
On his problems

Why had he come this way?
Why had he stopped?
Why had he taken
Responsibility
For this body?
Why could he not
Walk away from it
Now? Why was he become
Downcast himself
From another's problem?

No, he says to himself
This will not do!

I am trying to help
But I cannot allow
This to do me in
From my own purpose!
And a little notion
Hardly noticed scurries
Through a corner of his mind
Is my purpose really what
I thought?

As the young man
Frets
Strange things
Begin to happen
In the corpse
A kind of humming
Energy
Begins a diminutive roar
All sorts of tiny creatures
Working very hard
And gaining nourishment
From their labors
Work and work
Until not one
Speck
Of it remains

The young man can
Not believe his eyes
And rubs them thinking
Himself asleep
What was here
In front of him
Is no longer

As the mown hayfield
Sends up new
Shoots in its desire
To make seed
The pictures of what its
Stalks should look like
Strictly held in
Its being

So the forlorn
Dead body
Realizes
With alacrity
And dignity
Its final use

To think over this
Miracle of resolution
The young man lies down
Resting his head
On his hand
What was
Is no more
As it was
And becomes
Other things
All its parts
Disassemble
Are carried off
With precise knowledge
Of what to do

But he doesn't

Should he pick up
His backpack
Sling it on and
Trek forward to the
Sea?

Still running through his head
Is his vision-journey
So beautiful and
Inviting
What he saw and
Felt there
Appealed to him
Made him feel
Important

And to each
Contour of his body
The memory of the water
Surging by

Causes him to smile
Thinking of
Dolphins
Racing along beside
Laughing in the
Spray of bubble
Cascades

Intrusively
His images by themselves
Change
Into the small
Villages nestled
Below his mysterious
Mountains
Where his path took him
Early on
Where people work
Their gardens and
Go to church Sundays

A spikey bundle of nostalgia
Presents itself
Seeps into his
Awareness
Why those common places?
Why not the sea
Or the mountains
Themselves?

He has no way
Yet to answer himself

As he arises and
Gathers his things
A few loose stones
Drop from the waffled soles
Of his boots
Marking the place
Where he lay
He stands solemnly
Not making any sense
Out of it
Pondering his direction
Listening to his
Heart

THE THREE OF THEM

The three of them (a man and two women called
Spiritual, Hip and Lotus)
Make me a bower of pipes to sleep in.

I tiptoe around it, awed.

Only God can make my pavillion
Through me alone
Bit by bit
It scales the clouds.
Below, as it rises, the scaffold, obsolete,
Falls away.
The shaft, the column of support
From the rock
Gleams, stainless and ample
Amidst the tangle of weeds and lies

I stand at the leafy top
Pouring petals from my fingers
hearts of candy from my mouth
dew from my eyes
My pavillion is secure.
My vines are green and gold
The blossoms pink and orange.
It is above the trees but not on a hill.
From a valley between the hills it grows
Silversteel strong and wide.
There is room enough — who will join me?
Now there are doors in the column.
Children come and go, tasting.
I feed them grace and milk
grapes and ice cream
wine and snow

At once there is a roar
The hills fall away
Shattering, scattering to the abyss.

The seed falls into the cyn.
The people, in silken gowns and shifts
          tinted lemon, aqua, azure,
Cling squealing to the sides
Onto roots and tendrils
Bared.
Raw dirt smell, strong, wet, meaty,
Aromatic.
Skies heaving, ponderous brown, closing.

How can stars shine here?
And the moon?

A tolling bell
The village sheik
Is waiting on the quai of yore
The ships asea
A-whaling go
Are never seen no more

A-hai-li-ei
A-hai-li-o
Now easy onward
Play we so

Announce the mast seen far about
The way of all to
Go and come
One minor tune is played the shout
A tricklet singing at
The moon

Ya-ta-hai
Ya-ta-hei
Now easy onward
So we play

All singers wail
All habits broke
And here a vision from below
I know the song
I know the way
The wooly garment now to sew

Ya-ta-hai
Ya-ta-hei
Now easy onward
So we play

Ever if you had the peace
Would make amends
Across the sea
The sheik to win
And settle out
The breezes softly garnering

> *A-hai-li-ei*
> *A-hai-li-o*
> *Now easy onward*
> *Play we so*

The old people speak the words
And the words
Are becoming the mountains
And the mountains are speaking
The mud on the road and the wooden bridge
Where the old people turned to walk
                And not get splashed
The bridge over a dry wash, far below
A parade of old people
On the road. Rain, and snow
And now sun.
The hills say, Go, go up
Follow the road, and on the bridge
Rejoice ahead
The road there
On the other side
Is dry
And a stream flows beside it
Should you thirst.

The cars cannot go over
But turn off left to
Follow the muddy road.

Backwards
The vistas receding
We're speeding
Along a twilight path
Moon not risen

I look behind
To me ahead
Where we were
Rhythm of hoofbeats
Pulling away
Galloping

I am papoose
My eyes tear-blinded
By wind whipping
My blanket is loose
Tight-strapped secure
Only my eyes move
And they see only shadows

Not curled or cuddled
Here
Time for straight
Seclusion
Tenuous delusion
of world illusion
I sleep awake
I wakening
Sleep

The mountain peaks gleam and sparkle
Gifts to the eyes and heart
The big dog of heaven licks them clean
Wagging his feathered tail.
Eddying silver snowflakes
  Even in summer.

Glittering tower of steel and glass
I am moon-silver alloy
  Transmuted to purest light
Stretched tight

Rainbows leap from my myriad prismatic sides

My mirrors catch the lightning,
Toss it safely in my arms.
We josh and laugh in unison,
Singing a tune high out of mind
  Not a jungle tune
  This rhythm has the tenderest beat.

Through me worlds are formed
From me and of me as well
Made manifest
From the desire to become,
And to grow towards perfection

Not shattered fragments of a chalice
But discrete facets
As of a diamond
Raylets from a star

They are not dangerous to know

The beacon beckons softly
Shows the way to come
To the mountains
  Crisply aloof
  Gleaming
  Ghosts of everpresent glories
Resounding of ourselves

PART THREE

Can I be, on waking here again
Verging on an understanding of my
Problems with this place?
Is it a matter of surrender to its power?
See its deceptive serenity
Hear the meadowlark's fluted chortle
The chip of the wren on the cholla
See the dive of the swallow

Now my feelings are gossamer
Flitting in short waves
From plus to minus
Awe is inspired here
And anger
Why anger?

My wonder is not softened
Into fondness
It is still wonder, and awe
And breathtaking dazzlement

But this morning
At the entrance to the canyon
Buffalo Head Rock Canyon
(as I have named it)
I have caught it unawares

It is yawning and stretching
It has bleary eyes
Full yet of sand
The air moves now only
In a whisper
Caressing last year's grass stalks
Gracefully nodding their
Tiny banners and
Grama bush-curls

While from below in the dense
>*Pink soil*
Deep roots are sending
>*New green shoots forth*
>*Amidst the nursemaid protection*
>*Of the old, frizzled*
>*Bunch*

Juniper trees
Are you spitting off pollen
As you did that day
I watched from the hayshed
>*As the slantwise sunbeams caught*
>*Each puffed cloud*
>*Hanging expectantly*
>*With surprise that the air*
>*Was so still*

This morning these moments here suspend me

There is too much to see
>*Or know*
My gaze still searches for
>*My band of mares*
>*Flagged by the gleaming*
>*White rump of one or two*
Bunched or spread out
>*On the mesas across there*
>*South of the river*
>*Lounging, waiting*
>*An eye turned this way*
>*Now and again*
>*To watch the progress of the*
>*Feed truck*
>>*Has it started out from*
>>*The hayshed? Is the*
>>*Grain loaded?*

Flick of a tail in casual impatience
Mild stomp of hoof
> *Belly full anyway*
> *Why worry?*
> *Here comes my foal again to nurse*
>> *Nuzzle, butt my flank*
>> *I shift my weight to*
>> *Accomodate him*
>> *And nip his small tight-muscled*
>> *Rump*
>> *He humps up a little*
>> *Kicks and slurps*
>> *Contentedly*
> *We have a generous*
>> *And fine balance*
>> *Between us*
> *And love each other*
>> *Intently and dearly*
> *He is my fourth baby*
> *I have been so attached*
>> *Loving and caring*
>> *To them all*
> *I remember them all*
> *As any mother does*

These mesas and canyons and springs
Have so many secrets
An eternity is hidden here
> *As the band of horses*
> *Found themselves*
> *Innocently*
> *Clustered, quietly waiting*
> *Out their time*

> *Yes I miss them yes I miss them*
> *And all that they symbolize*

There is too much to see
The brain is dizzied by all the
Complex irregularity
> *Monotony*
It all looks about alike
> *From over here*
> *In its eco-layers*
>> *Bosque, river surfacing here and there*
>> *Bright rosy cliff*
>> *Grey-green meadow*
>> *Watersource canyons*
>>> *Springs, pools, cottonwoods*
>> *Interspersed darkgreen dots*
>>> *Juniper, piñon, cholla*
>> *Mesa level, wavy and humpy*
>> *Jagged black clump of Ortiz*

So, the grass here will grow
And the rain will fall and
The spirits will guide
> *The wind will blow*
> *The boulders will tumble sometimes*
> *The arroyos will fill and rush*
> *The coyotes will yip*
>> *And these birds will sing and*
>> *Raise their young*
All these things will happen
More now, that livestock
> *Bred to be used and sold*
Are absent, in large number

But what about the relationships
Of the ground and hoof,
The grass and the stomach?
> *Does it perhaps*
> *Yearn to be eaten*
> *To fulfill its purpose?*

Am I not meant to walk the earth
> *(Earth)*
In my many guises
To fulfill my purpose?

The land has things to tell me
And I am only beginning to listen

MORNING AT THE RANCH II:
MEMORIAL DAY

Morning's slipping in so soft
Pervasive aroma of olive blossoms
   Wafting up from the bosque
Peeping fingers of sunlight
Exploring my face
Inviting me to wake and see
Tree-foraging birds
Hear them chatter and call
They are most the same kinds
As at home in town
Linnet, tit, jay
Fearless phoebe clinging
To antenna on my van
Her curious head atilt
Viewing the shiny brown bush
Newly grown in her domain

The birds of evening here
Are nighthawks
Flyers in a class with
Swallows, gulls, falcons
They soar, hover, scan, swoop
With rolly-coaster screech
And braking roar of wings
In the bottom of their dives

What a pile of rocks
This eroded tableland
Not the Ortiz nor Cerrillos made this:
This is the spew of the
Mighty Jemez
Pebbled fragments
Sharp shatter-faceted
Some burnt

The Ortiz never broke through
What was once higher ground
    (Said the geologist)
Like the linear hogback intrusions
Revealed raw in this horizontal
Morning light
Juniper shadows long ovals
Elling to the west

Sharp-edged flat of mesaland
Northwest of here
La Bajada
Hard knife rim
Falling away to the Rio Galisteo

As I exploring walked about
Last evening, I found
Some places of the natives

My horses clambered these
Slippery rocked canyon walls
They knew the springs
And the best eating places
Lush little grassy meadows tucked in
Bends and shady curves of the arroyos
In the fall they'd munch
Russian Olive berries
They'd crowd together into the
Junipers for noon siestas
Out of the high sun
Or lounge close into a cliff

As close to wild as I
Could give
Mares, yearlings, stallions
They knew their needs
Became strong and purposeful
The freer they were
The more affectionate

They loved my visits
    (When I could find them)
Coming in turns to be
Petted and crooned over

When the time came the
Lead mare signalled in some manner
And down to water or fresh grass
They'd go, hard hoofs clippetting
What muscled backs and legs
Had they
What calm, assurance, joy

*

The first of them "let out" – an event
Of glee and trepidation for us all –
Half a dozen fillies
A trailerload
Halters off! in the riverbottom
Inside the lower gate
Such dainty steps, such sniffing
A quick eye back to us
For final permissive understanding
Then a proud and haughty
Exuberant spring into the unbelievable
Down the river they sprinted
Off out of view
So fast they ran
In their birthright realization
And remembrance
Of the freedom they always
Knew was theirs

The foal knows his wildness
As he struggles from your grasp

They do not have to live
Like this
To this extreme
As indeed most horses
Appreciate human care
And affection
Not really minding the
Stall and paddock

But they know who they are
These old grounds are their habitat
Born eons past on the plains
Given the need and pleasure
To run and call
And know each other in the
Secret ways
Of all herd creatures

Or, in turning out these
Individuals to the river or
Up here on the mesas
Was I freeing each spirit
Newborn? Was it a real surprise
That fences went on and away
So very far? Was it as automatic
And effortless as it seemed?
This is of course true:
They were suddenly free
As a skywatcher bird
Having to search their
Own livelihood
Not hand-fed in a field
They became responsive to their
Own selves and their place

Not losing themselves forever
Or getting torn or broken
Or eaten by lions
Their response to the open
Was all good

The whole summer they fed exclusively
On fodder they found
They were fat and sleek
Independent
Truly alive
They respected and knew
Their world
Intimately
Were gracious, tolerant, relaxed
They performed their rituals
Chose their leaders
Understood their needs and
Claimed their heritage
Not as a privilege won
But as an immemorial way of being

I had forgotten why

It's been said by others and
I did think I had done
So many things here
With unnecessary abandon
Headstrong lady
Spending herself rashly, living
Foolishly, whimsically, impulsively

But as I now view this land
And think on the things
I allowed
I caused to happen here
And realize that for a short time
These few animals
Now cared for by others
In other ways, other places
Knew in these lifetimes
Theirs and mine
The honor of the natural ways
I can finally say
That was my dream, my reason

They let it happen so easily
Their consciousness was so
Attuned here, so complete

I had forgotten why
It was so important

Yes, I too can live here
Or anywhere
If I need to
For a while
For as long as it takes
To let the knowledge
Seep into my bones
Longer than it took the horses
But not so different
Let it tell me of my heritage
For I too have walked
Mesas like these
And walk them now in other feet.

To carry over this integration
Is the key
To at-one-ment

MORNING AT THE RANCH IV:
RIDGE ROAD ABOVE ANNIE GREEN SPRING

Last part of June and
Still cold mornings
Woke from the chill
And bundled on the
Mississippi quilt

Black black sky
Speckled over completely
Myriad stars misted
With lightning clouds
Subdued sleepy city to north

Looked up again and surprise
Crescent moon hanging
Spilling over northeast dark
Balanced by Venus
Holding the reins

Soon came first light
So tentative I wondered
If it was just moonglow
Then clumpy bushes
Appeared like ghosts
And the reddest
Streak across the horizon
Reaching a pink and lavender
Trellis over my mesa

I then went back to sleep

Why describe dawn?
It happened and I witnessed
Extraordinary dawn
Removed from this sunlit
Breeze-tossed morning
By the soft relaxation
Of sleep

Right on schedule
Ordinary and unique
Break of day
Dividing the night world
Of moon, stars and mystery
  Strange messages
  Coded secrets
And daytime
Active with doing
Like writing things down
Trying to remember
  Decipher
  Understand

All the things
That happen at night

My notes are full of hints
And I want to know why, for instance,
The wine leapt dancing
Whirling from my cup, spilling
Four times last evening
It gained motion
As from a centrifuge
Spurting like a reverse tornado

What kind of energy
Was I, or something,
Giving the cup
To make it flow thus?
And this morning I
Found spilled water
Under the ice chest
Did I not secure the drain?

Yesterday I hiked down
Unerringly
To the spring below this
Trail
Where the wire mesh
Encloses what I guess
To be a grave
And found water
Grasses and clover
Rock-knobbed overhang
Scant stream

I went to collect
Enough for my solar
Waterbag
But the pools were
Full of tadpoles so I
Left it be and
Followed the canyon on down
Hoping, again, to find
My scarf
Tied to a juniper years ago
When my love and I
Walked that way
Scarf left as a marker
The mark is gone but
The spring remains
And I find it easily now
Without the mark

Can I find the meaning
Of dreams and fragments
Without their markers?

For what else are
The figures of dreams
But hints to lead us
To the springs
Of our self-canyons?
How many springs
And how many arroyos
In a soul?
Many more than are
On this land

Or stars in the night sky

From what unknown depths
And directions do they
Flow?
Disguised or
Displayed
Recessed or
Revealed
Convoluted or
Day-plain?

MORNING AT THE RANCH V:
PHOTO: THE NEGATIVE

Visited, oddly, by a hummingbird
I awaken abruptly at my camp
No flowers here, too dry
No red plastic feeder dangling
Red sun yes; veiled ball of new flame

Hanging on the northeast horizon
Over the mounds of the Sangres
All is shrouded in suspension of dust
I can see only fifty miles

It is thirsty on the mesas – shrivly
Bunches of grasses, crumpled and subdued
Crunch dryly underfoot
Waft of dawn air surprisingly cool

O where is the fruited plain?
It is seven and it is morning but
Would Browning not call this place
Morocco? Not England, for sure

Mysteries of the desert: this inhospitable land
A fascination to the artist
What does it call up to us, in us?
What portions of our wholeselves bleed-through?

Does one embrace it, call it 'mine'?
Hardly, for it rebuffs, and hides, and smiles its
Sphinx smile. It dares you not
Merely displays its monotonous tawny shroud

Broad and convolute, washed sandy
Spreading tease of the undersea world it was
Mirror of the restlessness and violence
Of the blandly grinding waves

Meticulously arranged scenic balance
And the scene is not itself
The rhythms delight, inspire, recall
Not Beethoven as Colorado, but a subtler voice

Quality of end-of-civilization-as-we-know-it
Towards which we, innately knowing,
Shape our selves
As the flower shapes the stem and the leaves

Or perhaps the seed beckons the seed
In perpetual spiral, mimicking the greater
Grand rising circles of the lesser
And the greater, the sequence of the flow

Here, abundance withheld, yet displayed abundantly
Lies in a magick of forms repeated, repeated
Barebones seen so widely, so a-roundly
Integrated into these high places

The oceans came and went, come and go
In the great respiration
Patterns and cycles inscrutable
Carrying us, allowing us glimpses

Panorama of rocks, sands, clay
Laid wide, raw and richly adorned
Dazzling, de-focussing our eyes with glittering
Sunmotes reflecting the great fire

Not exposed but unfolding
Unrevealed but apparent
In creases, caves, scoured canyons
Where dinosaurs nested once in swamps

We are offered, from time to time
Enrichment entering our lives
From people, events, things, places
Translated according to our own mind-spaces

And to what we can presently accept
Remaking ourselves in the moment
Selecting evernow by our action
Mental and physical in response

To the special significance
Of what we create in our surroundings:
Here, this desert, demonstrating the
Vastness, and incredible variety

Open within the integrity of its sameness
Reaching in the great extravagant arcs
Of our visual and emotional fields
Gives us the very chapter and verse

Of our choices within the boundaries
Of our selected form of being
Helps us remember the unity of our soul
The balance, artistry, creativity of our
Eternal, momentary existence

REFLECTIONS ON ROSE QUARTZ

High-summer nightfall on the mesa
Already earlier
Late into July, warm and breezy
A shade below eighty, I'd guess
Too cool to need a swim
Too warm, as we used to say
For a sweater

When we all lived
Together
We overflowed our spaces
Our fountains splashed
Our pools quivered and rippled
Fish flickered
Dogs wagged, parties gloried
Warm times, those old days
Humid with swamp-sweat
Easy-moving
Sometimes the sultriness stifled
As became that lifestyle
We grew it out

I think it might be raining
In the Jemez
I hear it's raining down
In Arkansas
The sun dallies on either side
Of the solstice
And soon, now Leo's here
Will plunge headlong
Flaming
Toward equinox

Oh pink luminous sky
Violet, gold-ray'd
Layers of thick grayness
Obscuring the horizon
I sit on a rock in this
Pygmy forest
Surrounded by fragmentations
Spewed in times past
By yonder old fire-face
Transformed
To diffuse cobalt
Azure
Indigo-shadowed

You, sky, are the same blanket
That covers us all
Leapt from that trade-place
Poked through with stars
And aspirations
Full and empty
With mountains and hopes

Send your lights and your
Rainbows
Lead the young to pass gently the old
Inspire, unite
Leave us not awestruck
But turned in the spiral
A notch more up
As we spin in this dusk
Away from our sun
In this Leo time
We shall sustain and supplant
What is begun
Build, grow, and laugh
And become pure gold light
The glow of the fire whirling in us
Restored
Banked
Ever available

PART FOUR

A tap on your shoulder
> *Who is there, who is there?*
> *Reaching across timeless sands*
> *Speaking strange sidewise scripts*
> *Nodding, beckoning as you turn*
> *Come away, love, come around*
> *Over here, and see the other views*

A gentle nudge in your ribs
> *Playful and cool, who is there?*
> *Hum of a bee in lateflowers*
> *Who are you looking for, in your*
> *Dreams, who goes away, beyond*
> *Time when you waken?*
> *Over here, and see the other views*

A waft of air along your arm
> *Who is there in the woods?*
> *What is on the other side of those*
> *Rows of trees? More trees?*
> *Easy, now, easily listen to*
> *Birdsong, the last of the young hummers*
> *The drooping blossom in its fullness*

A warm touch, fingers through your hair
> *Who is there, who is there?*
> *Phantom lover, known from before*
> *Soothing, calming, caressing*
> *Call me again when the leaves*
> *Shout gold and fall amber*
> *And the trees stand bare*

A soft whisper, do you hear
> *Who is there, calling me?*
> *Clouds of crystals sliding west*
> *Ships of the morning catching light*
> *Not yet come to the garden of love*
> *The patterns stand still so slow they float*
> *I wait, and the sun is here*

We are not all-wise, who've gone before
        But come and go and are
        Seen again in this world
        As round and round the seasons turn
        From the mouths of the messengers
        Echo words with flowing feathers
        Over here, love, and see the other views

And then you came to me
One day as I lay dream-awake
Waiting in a quiet time
Still a stranger in the land

You walked from the south along the beach
Your feet slicing the lapping wavelets
As always watching for fish
Flashing in the hollow of the breaker

I sat on the sand
Gazing at the blue-gray horizon
When I noticed you come near
I watched you approach, smiling

And I saw your dear face, restored
Your eyes glowing clear and deep
For you now remember the secrets
Of all things, and that my soul

Which I clutched to myself before
And now show you so willingly
Knows the light and the darkness
And that it is all the same

You stood before me in this place
Saying not a word
Telling me things I had forgotten
And things that are to be

And that I already and always am
Myself the hand of God

PASTORAL

I've heard the definitive sixth
I'm walking round the hill
Round fat hill like the lump of clay
On the wheel; my spiral path
Like the potter's finger-trails shaping

In strange lands shall I sing
My Christmas hymns
My season of solstice
Walking round my hill
My sturdy rich fat hill

I walk around step by step
As round and round I go
The black and white horse with his
Round rich buttocks
Follows me, willingly
To the strange lands of Christmas
Even further
The lightning dances about our shoulders
The richness springs beneath our feet

And round and round stretches straight
Out into infinity
Stretches as tough haunches
Dig shod hooves into rain-
Drenched soil, wildflower'd
Stretches straightaway
Unexpectedly
As I solo
He so strong could carry me easily
Across rich mountain meadows
Yet I walk ahead, alone
And it is good

A Dream

*A couple comes along and occupies an ovoid space
in my dwelling. They give me a snake which I place
in a tree, where she eats insects and sleeps. She
hangs there as if dead. I think she is dead, and
mourn. She is in cooperative captivity, however,
and as I turn away, I see that she has given
birth to hundreds of babies which crawl off along
the sides and corners of my large room, and out
and away to where they need to go.*

*

*The little grey snake
Climbs frantically
In the chamisa
To escape me and FüFü
Turning, slithering
I gently pry her loose
Untangle the foot-long
Footless coils of warm skin
Nestled restlessly now
Frightened in my palm
Carry her to a brushy place
In the corner of the yard
She springs from my hand
Disappears in the
Shrubbiness*

*

*Six, the morning plateau
Not yet morning
The hour from which
To leap
To become morning-seven
That hour between
An expansion, suspension
A pause of blood
Between heartbeats
Nothing is required*

*

*What is required policy on
Rattlesnakes? asks the man
Mowing the fields*

*

*Snakes of garden, field, and dream
Wounded, threatened, burgeoning
Michael's axe of legend
Hacking, slicing
Killing that odd, shapely
Rope, that thread of
Intelligence
Coiled up in a basket*

*The tiny ones hop off like
Frogs so quick they slither
Away to their corners of the world
To lurk under bushes and watch
For the passerby*

*And I, in my thrashing, could not see
What the snake in his delicate
    Intuitive propensity
Facilely removes:
    The ropes part
    For his gentle passage
What tightens on my wrist is
    To him a stepping stone
Graced precision guides his arrow-limned
    Convoluted path*

*No more:
As the snake knows his hole
I am at home in the rooms
    Of my being
Secure
And the things of this world
    Come and go*

I have waited

In this world I need the birds
    Careening in this morning sky
    Trees thrusting past my window
    Snakes wriggling in the grass
In my inner world
    I am they, and they are me
    We are the same

When the snake dies, his leaving
    Causes no alarm
His flesh is consumed
His cells transformed
    In nature's way

I
Shall turn into air and water
    Cover the globe
    Travel, in my mind-parts
    Widely
Ideas, emotionforms, and balm
Spirit foods will spring from me

As the snakelets stream away
    In profusion
    Their paths directed, ordained
My offspring
    Will fly through barriers and
    Around corners to reach you

Where we shall merge and conjoin
    Not as before, in mere resemblance
    But mingling our very ions
Then, at the same non-insistent
Moment, one of those between 6 & 7
    One of those without the
    Urgency of this world
We shall together know our wholeness
    Our holiness
Together in the arms of the great
Peace called Love
Unbound and unboundaried

We shall soar gathered in the
        Endless instants
        All of us
Bathed in the black light
Of all and nothing
Knowing the fullness and richness
Recognizing Job's choice
        And Mary's Lamb

*Cynthia Grenfell lived her early
years in New Rochelle, New York.
She left Vassar College, where
she majored in Theatre, to marry
and move to Arkansas, eventually
engaging in ranching there and
in New Mexico. She now makes
her home in Santa Fe, and
is currently working on a novel
and a series of dream-poems.*